To All The Ones I've Left Behind

Vania Copeland

To God Be the Glory

Uncle Vilas,
Thank you.

Contents

Dear Reader,

Praise the Lord!

This work is extremely special to me. My prayer is that it ministers to you, in the way that its contents have ministered to me.

These poems are not my assumption of knowing everything or even my assertion that I understand everything. However, when I am going through anything - joy, pain, change, excitement, love - I write, so you are getting inside access to my heart and mind. These pieces are truly birthed from a multitude of moments and people.

The time it took me to complete this work can be blamed on a mixture of my own self-doubt breeding procrastination, my choice to heal, as well as other choices of mine waiting their turn to be made. The hardest choice to make was definitely to keep going - despite the time passing, despite doubtful thoughts- and to hang on to what I know my Father God has told me. He promised to command a blessing in all I set my hands to in Deuteronomy 28:8, and because I know God is not slack on His promises I committed to sit down and complete this work.

Within, you will find three parts: part 1: Put God First, Part 2: The Sappy Friend, and Part 3: Ms. Energizer Bunny. Each part holds its own purpose.

Part 1 is easily explained; it is imperative to put God first in all that we do. There's a verse in Colossians 3:23 KJV which states,

"...whatsoever ye do, do it heartily, as to the Lord...". Part 1 takes this verse and runs with it. Without the grace of God, nothing would be able to be done at all. It is in our heavenly Father that we live, move, and have our being, so it is only right for me to dedicate my work to him - from the opening. In moments where I needed extra direction, God would give me a new poem, or a new song, and Part 1 is a product of those moments. When I originally sat down to write them, I didn't know I'd later take the time to collect them for this work. Nonetheless, I am thrilled to share how God spoke to me, delivered me, and made me new with you all.

Part 2: The Sappy Friend, is a nod to the countless times I've been referred to as "sappy", or "lovey-dovey" from my associates. I believe in the importance of telling my friends, family and significant others what they mean to me. Each moment together we have on this earth is a gift, I don't believe in taking any of them for granted. I deeply value people for their uniqueness, their idiosyncrasies, and their significance, and this spills out of me often. When I'm not pouring this appreciation into the people around me, I fill up my notes app! (That app has seen every side of me.) As time has gone on, the notes app and various notebooks have caught the brunt of my emotions. However, for Part 2 I picked the poems that were from more pivotal exchanges and equally pivotal choices.

Part 3: Ms. Energizer Bunny, comes from the way my mother used to refer to me as such. She'd call me that bunny because well, I am pretty talkative. As a kid, I would talk her ear off. I think she loved it. She often tells me, "If we were in school at the same time you and I would be friends. I just know it." Besides when she really needs the time to recharge, I'm pretty sure she loves speaking with me...right mom? Either way, this part is comprised of my thoughts on topics that didn't quite fit into the "lovey dovey" category of Part 2 or the "Souled out" flavor of Part 1.

With that being said my friend, let's dive in.

Enjoy and God bless you!

With all my love,

Vania Copeland

I heard God say,

"Always keep going"

"The way of the faithful is committing to pay the price, even if the cost cannot be known. And trusting that, in the end, it will be worth it."

- QUEEN REGENT MIRIEL (THE RINGS OF POWER)

Part 1: Put God First

My Big Brother

I'm not bringing you all a fairy tale
What I must tell
Really happened and it tends to compel
So, sit back and listen as I describe with detail
The life of my big brother, you may know him as well

One night two thousand years and some change ago
My big Brother fulfilled a commitment denying his ego
He set fear aside and took no thought for his life

And sometimes my heart aches and I wonder
What ran through his head, while he climbed to his fate
Despising shame in my stead
But mostly I am filled with gratitude, I remember to fix my attitude, elevate my altitude,
And read to increase my aptitude

Are you grasping the pure magnitude
Trust me when I tell you
My big brother still shines bright
And while he walked the earth he was the truest light
And if you don't yet then believe me for the bruises
Who else could stay committed in the face of false accusers?

But an older sibling with real love will help you like that
They'll take the beatin' while you the true offender get the slack
They know we wouldn't
Be able to handle the wrath of mom and dad nor that whoopin
So, they humble their hearts and take our portion of the pie
And even with the weight of that sacrifice we still keep coming up

shy

Nevertheless, my big brother led with providence
A man of faith, love, joy, peace, long-suffering and goodness

And this is just the start of the story
My brother did so much
But for time's sake I must sum it up
Living by faith as the just
He gave our Father his trust
He sacrificed and didn't lose
He left but wasn't gone
He fell and then he rose
And now he has a throne.

Change

This skin is too tight,
There's no room to grow.
Smothered in this atmosphere of fear,
Dejected by one glance in the mirror.
Where's the girl with the brilliant smile?

I don't see her.

Unrecognizable, unidentifiable, indiscernible,
Are you that impressionable?
Opposite of just doing it, oooo girl please don't.
Skin losing the glow of life as your lungs' supply you continue to
deprive.

Babygirl, can't you see that pull is a lie?

Dip your toes into the pool of life
Take a drink from a well never dry
Replenish that sparkle in your eye
Change right now before you die.

I Entered a Staring Contest with The Moon

I entered a staring contest with the moon.
She won.
I looked away.
She's a pro at this.
I couldn't help but get lost in her presence.
I felt her godliness.
Then wondered if she was God's presence.
Let's think about this.
I mean she's there all the time.
Even when we can't see her,
She's there on time.
And even in our darkest nights
She's there the whole time.
And even when we start to sink
She pulls back the tide.
Are you picking up the theme of this rhyme?

My Heavenly Father said he'd never leave nor forsake me.
Even when I lost my grip his son was there to save me.
And when I call on Jesus, He moves closer to me
And when I surrendered all he came to live within me
And now I spread the good news to whoever was born to hear me
And now I spread the good news to whoever is dying to hear me
And now I spread the good news to whoever knows they need me
And now I spread the good news to whoever believes though they
can't see me

I show myself strong to those that know me
I want them to know now is the time they have to seek me

And if you hesitated here's something else for you to believe me
God is there all the time
And even when you can't see him
He's there on time
And even in our darkest nights
He's there the whole time
And even when we start to sink
He'll pull back the tide
And now he's asking you to look to his light

Don't look away

HOME

As a child I always felt slightly out of place
Just a bit unsafe
I could never shake the feeling that I was waiting
Not realizing my inner being remained in a dormant state
While the rest of me was in disarray
I could never cry too long or stay angry
I never even bothered to make a birthday wish
When I closed my eyes to appease those around me
I knew a blown out candle wouldn't bring me what I most needed
With every party, every year I felt unresolved
I knew I wasn't home
I could hear a faint call
As time went on the voice grew louder

Finally, and not by chance, I found a consuming fire
I was baptized in the Spirit and awoken with power
I felt myself soar to new heights and saw the tops of skyscrapers
I could see between the colors and hear butterfly wings flutter
I flew with them for a little while 'til somewhere below me I felt
my body quaver
With a peace unlike any I ever felt before
I had absolution and found the solution to the greatest illusion
The price for my debt was paid with grace in blood
Making room for atonement to fall sweetly at the behest of
Repentance
This was a free gift and all I had to do was believe
In Faith, I called on the name of someone I had never seen
Then, Jesus led me home to the Father of lights.
Under the shadow of The Almighty, abiding in secret place of the

Most high

Redeemed

I'm redeemed and so free. I love it beneath your wings.
You inspire new songs to sing, with gratitude my voice rings.
I'm compelled to let your light show
Urged to let others know
I can not let my life go by
and neglect to testify
You lifted me out of the mud, washed me off
Made me new and changed my name, despite the cost.
My past is forgotten leverage
And expansion continues through this message

With your spirit
I'm in control of my soul
No longer in the passenger seat
No longer standing by
Now able to live by
A standard laid out on high

I'm redeemed and so free, the world barely recognizes me
They say "there's something about you"
and that's the perfect segue to tell them all about You
My tongue is a ready instrument
My hand a willing pen
To proliferate your boundless love
For more lives to begin

Stiff Where?

I'm no longer bound by the doubts and fears of others
I'm no longer bound by what makes them feel right
I had to shake off those chains
Because it's time for the Lord to reign
There's no accident in the way you created me
You know I will scream your name unabashedly.

Paradigm Shift

Everything is God.
God is good.
There is no bad.

Inspire

My tongue has the power to speak life
My tongue has the power to cause death
My tongue can be tamed by no man
Yet your Spirit oh my God

The same Spirit that raised Jesus
Helps guide my words with a quickening zest
I yield to the Comforter extinguishing the fire within my lips
Inspired by this Holy Spirit my tongue is liberation, articulating
God's faultless will for His creation.

It Took Time 1

Whole time I was naming what I felt pain, while its proper name is, change.

Uncomfortability waits for us in a new day.

Uneasiness sits patiently in the office of new opportunity.

Resistance keeps these undead states employed.

Welcoming the novel,

Embracing what was once held by tomorrow,

We become in step with the rhythm of evolution.

In this presence is fullness of joy.

To All The Ones I've Left Behind

To all the ones I've left behind. I'm not sorry:
I am rejoicing.
You may scorn me for no longer wishing to contort myself for you, but I have no ounce of remorse.
I lost years to the pursuit of your happiness.
Instead of taking all this time my God has given me to fill myself with Him, my desire to yield to you left me almost completely empty.
Yet like the song says, I never lost my praise.
I use my hallelujah to lift me higher.
Every morning I declare sweet blessings to my heavenly Father and ride His wings as I to learn to fly

It is impossible for me to justify any sort of sadness towards this elevation.
I outright refuse to mitigate my elation.
It has been God's plan for me all along, and it is my true desire.
To all the ones I've left behind, I'm throwing you into the fire.
It's no wonder the soul is dead without the Spirit of God giving it life.
Its dark requests are lethal, so I'm bringing them to the light.
To all bondage, addiction, depression, foul words, anxiety, lying, omission,
Manipulation, fornication, emulation, and idolization, consider this my resignation
No. I can't keep it simple.
I no longer choose to inflame this temple.

To all the ones I've left behind, accept your departure from my

ways.
I am an emblem of praise.

Surrender

Surrender isn't the same for everyone
I had to learn what it meant for me

Submission doesn't come easy for everyone
I had to see it was grace making it possible for me

Sacrifice isn't appealing to everyone
I must choose daily to embrace the freedom it brings for me

Sanctification doesn't last for everyone
I need it to last a lifetime for me

Something about Jesus doesn't excite everyone
I can't help but to feel grateful he was born, lived, died, rose and
ascended for me.

Identity

If you knew who you were
You would put me first
You'd reach out for me
In spite of what you see

The Difference

Unlike the sea
Yielding to the sand
I live lawlessly and free at my Father's right hand

Unlike a cloud
Dismembered by rain
I am whole through Christ who shall remain

The Light of Life

There was a woman who was filled with darkness
What she touched perished, and nothing grew within her

Then by the will of God Friday brought Love her way
Love ever so graciously took her by the hand

In awe of this unique being, she opened her heart to him.
Love poured inside her and birthed a river with no end

She was so full of love and yet she was now light
The light became her life and Love never left her side

Part 2: The Sappy Friend

Evanescent

With just one look

I see all of
    you

I wrestle against my better judgement

It tells me to look

    away

As much as I want to

Take in all of
    you

I succumb to the benevolence within

It's best to stay

    away

Time

Time keeps moving,

but that's fine,

It's bringing me closer to you.

Every Season I'll Remember You

As the calm light of day shines and the first eager yet meek snowflakes hurry to the ground,
they create crystalline pathways of frost glittering amidst a white field
laying just as undisturbed as my memory of your voice.
The way it growls and rolls from your throat moments after you've just awoken,
With purpose I place my head to your chest
To feel your intention rumble
Climbing its way to our ears.
On the hottest summer day
When the sun stalls in the sweltering sky
As I race to the sea seeking sanctuary for my scorched soles
I recall the heat your gaze coerced to my cheeks without protest
Your eyes singled me out and reassured me.
They shined as you peered into my collection of stories,
Picking out your favorite and chronicling my proclivities.
You warm me from the inside out underneath your scrutiny.
You showed me what it meant to be loved for what makes me, me.
Our time with each other mirrors the rhythm of creation,
Yet this year as the seasons changed, they altered our association

No music *clap clap clap clap*

I didn't even notice until now

We didn't listen to any music the whole time

Every melody I needed played in your eyes

I was completely hooked on you

And you knew it.

Outdated

Someday someone is gonna say trends from this year are outdated

One day this summer's heat wave won't be talked about

Today the footprints I left in the sand last week are gone

Yesterday a stranger told me good morning, yet they've already forgotten my face

With all the ways time can wipe away every detail of a day in its sprint forward

I could never forget the details of your face

The memory of your touch will never truly be gone

The lessons you've taught me will always be talked about

Our love this summer will never become outdated.

 Then You

I lived life in my own unique way

Now I've met you

And I can't seem to picture the rest without

You

The In Between

For thousands of years people have been drawn to the in between
There's a time nuzzled betwixt the day and night
While some rest and some arise
Where it's not quite yesterday nor the promise of tomorrow
And the morning light has yet to deliver joy for scattered sorrow

In this hour filled with opportunity
The untouchable free-will takes steps towards perpetuity
Every choice we make has a separate destination
Some choose to be rash others are riddled with hesitation
While the mind deliberates, and the brain calculates
Becoming tepid as it meanders to evaluate
There's no time for getting lost in regret
While the soul anticipates what it doesn't have yet

Frequently it's pondered how easily life could be different
Had there have been more intelligence
But in the doorway before you, I hold no pessimistic sentiment
My life before I walked through the sill was filled with merriment
I spent my days fulfilling the goal to inspire
And danced through nights on dreams of flying higher
I let the sun pirouette off my collar bones
And intently pursued the moon's brilliance when it shone
Like a firebird I rose from ashes of past lives
And insisted on sparking fervent change with melodic battle cries

With all the hues of peace I've seen, there's one that is so bold
There's no denying my curiosity with this brief threshold
The beats that lie between our greeting
The pulse of energy exchange that could have been fleeting
Choice brings me kaleidoscopic realms of possibility

As I admire the moments before our chapter in this story

A magnetic dance of calming delight
When in so many words I said you're Mr. Right
Then you held out your hand to affirm the assumption
I have to let you know, I spend time in this junction
& It's not because I wish I didn't reel you in
Or that I can even deny the inevitability of seeing you again
There's no room nor reason for resenting
The pull towards your smile and its timely glinting

I'm fully immersed in the gratitude of our choices
& praise God for the way He poised us
In the window of us colliding, and I suspect
Our appreciation will increase within the beauty of retrospect
While meditating on the moments before you stepped on the scene
I marveled at serendipity in our in between

Seeking

As we parted ways we wondered if we'd ever see each other again.

Now, I look for you everywhere I go.

Yktv

They say "when you know you know"

And boy don't I know.

Passerby

When I saw you, I got butterflies

And I'm looking for a way to ratify

Like real life justify

Wanting you so badly

And you're just a passerby.

It Took Time 2

Time is fascinating.

Who told her what I needed?

How did she know to bring you back now?

Everything is up.

Except for our time.

I Gave it All to the Sea

I knew to give the sea what was left
I knew she could carry it
I knew it would last in her
I knew there was no longer room for it in me
I knew she'd hold the memories
I knew when she rolled in again with a promising touch
She'd take them to their rightful place in this plane
I knew she'd let the laughter and joy sparkle in response to the sun upon her waves
I knew she'd allow our jokes to add force to her undulations
I knew the sea could use our love to nurture her inhabitants
I knew she'd infuse it within the way she brought calm to anyone lost in her on purpose
I knew she'd let it diffuse into those that sought solace in her dependency,
Although she may recede,
I knew her return with the love I poured into her would provide others an ambience of never-ending romance
I knew I'd still think of you
I knew I'd miss every ounce of us
I knew our spark was genuine
I knew I could use the sea as a conduit
I knew she would keep our passion alive
Because I know when it's real, it can never die.

Raindrops

I was grateful for the rain, it hid the difficulty of walking away from you.

Adoration

You hold within your eyes a beauty I've never imagined
The lines denoting your smile tell of joy you've shared in abundance
The contentment in your lips speak of the peace the world needs
The deep certain timbre of your voice swells a melody similar to the waters barreling down on the sand
You may never wholly grasp the measure of my admiration
You were created by the same voice which manifested the earth see
Fearfully and wonderfully each of the complexities of your countenance came to be
Respect and awe are due a being of your distinction
Let not my words bring about any level of confusion!
First in my life comes the praise and exaltation of the Most High.
This is what allows me to recognize the blessing when you happened by
Chance is something I don't believe in so come on and drown in this adoration.

Windows

They say the eyes are windows to the soul
If I look in yours what will I behold
Will I see someone who's also waiting
for a precious love that will last?
Have you let the light in despite the
relentless attempts at snuffing out your glow?
I look in and you look out, do we see the same?
I've wanted to sit and gaze through
your windows since the moment I learned your name.

I Wish It Would Rain

I wish it would rain.
Not for the trees, but for me.
I want the earth to feel the force of the tears
That won't fall from my eyes.

I wish the atmosphere and I bore a contrast
But we are both dry.
I wish the sky was on my side right now.
I wish it would rain.

Divine

I watch the way you use your hands as they emphasize the words coming from the depths of you

Notice the spark behind your eyes as you recall the beauty of your legacy

Absorb the sincerity in your voice as you admit adoration without using those three little words

Quickening my pulse when you peer into my soul and I bare it in the open for you

I feel no need to hide from you

Your presence is spiritual

Although I've laid out a material map of the reverberations

Resulting from the frequency of our vibrations

It don't stop there

I'm aware of that zeal beneath your skin

I am akin to what blazes within

Now that you and I have managed to undulate along the same wavelength let's ride this rhythm

Allow it to continue flowing

As the natural syncs with the psyche

And the psyche ignites the divine

The brilliance has the tendency to alter whoever comes near

You are just right

And I'm so glad you're here.

11:11

Never believed in making wishes,

but I pray for you every time the door opens.

To love on me

I melt into your milk chocolate eyes and fold into your gaze.
I've taken up residence
in your perception.
Completely surrounded by your inspection
I feel free
when you take time out of your day to love on me.
My heart beats in rapture and I dutifully remember to capture, the way
your actions show your conviction
I feel heard
When you take time out your day to love on me

You celebrate my stretch marks, you dance down all my curves.
You honor my form with pure affection
I feel seen
when you take time out of your day to love on me.
Each time we are together,
You inspire my heart to tenderize,
you are my every desire personified.
I unapologetically crave and wholly cherish you.
In this dream
I feel serene
when you take time out of your day to love on me.

When No One Was Around

Ever since you,

I think about that tree falling when no one was around.

You made the air move differently,

To me you made a sound.

Part 3: Ms. Energizer Bunny

Night v. Light

We were taught to fear the dark
If our parents never asked us if we were sure we wanted our night light's
on. We would have never needed to say yes every time
If the movie never put the monster in the closet at night
We wouldn't have thought to stay up all night looking into the crack in
the closet door, imagining those keen and crooked yellow eyes looking
back at us.
If they never told us the boogie man lived under the bed
We wouldn't be afraid to let our legs over the edge while we slept.
And if the thieves didn't come at night
We wouldn't clutch our covers to a houses moan,
when it's just doing its best to stay upright
Not that they were wrong to caution us about the things going bump in
the night.
People choose the darkness to hide the parts of them that aren't right
They creep around in the hours where we lack our best sight
Malevolent opportunity consumes them in the dark,
they take advantage of the lack of clarity.
To them no light equals a lack of culpability
We must be wiser than those who feast on our vulnerability,
The absence of transparency,
The illusion of serenity,
As they choose insidious entropy.
Not so we can be hyper aware and clutch our covers
As our eyes dilate desperately
searching for light.
Rather,
I believe we must realize they're hiding from the light
so as the light we can fight
Forsaking all fear even at night
Rejoicing, and praising the Most High

engaging in warfare lacking any fright
As we keep present in our minds,
everything will be alright.

Sincerity

At the top of a pier,
with a breathtaking view of the city at night,
you looked into the broken parts of me
and wove them together with
a simple yet potent phrase.

You deserve to be loved.

That moment has stayed with me well beyond that night.
Although we no longer share our energy
I believed then and now you were right.
But it wasn't the words that healed me,
it was your sincerity.

Falling Down Hurts

Falling down hurts
But what is worse
the pain of hitting the ground or a wound that festers
when you refuse to get back up?
Would you rather that mistake be a blessing or your curse?
Would you like all your efforts to be disposed of,
because you'd rather lay in the dirt?
Is that how little your time and effort is worth?
Or how about the ideas you have yet to birth?
the work you have yet to work?
the firsts you have yet to unearth?
this is a concern you've refused to let be heard
before you can reach your grand goals
you have to learn how to get back up after you've been hurt

Roses

Roses aren't always red.

Say Sumn'

I want someone who can freely tell me what it is about me that has them
loving me.
Why do you keep me around.
I want someone to look in my eyes and feel excited to see me in the
morning.
Ask me how I'm doing and tell me the ways I make their heart skip or
something.
Like I'm just asking you to express yourself so I can feel better.
I woke up sad.
I want to know what it is about me that has you into me.
And before you say anything about not wanting to all the time
please consider how I'm feeling.
I just wanna know what it is about me that you love and appreciate.
Please.
Not a hard request if there are real things.
Just say sumn'.
-

Well my mama raised me to say nothing if I don't have something nice to
say
I may have embraced that to extreme levels but
See what's all inside of me is all hard to distinguish
My intentions formed out of relief and leisure
A short sighted choice led to momentous pleasure
And I could sit here and tell you all the reasons I have you here
But with all the pain in my heart I've forgotten how to hear
Hear the love hear the sweet words
Hear the difference in my heart's beat since you walked into my world
I can't tell you anything nice cause I have nothing nice to say
Every time I go to express these things to you I am blocked by all the pain
and dismay

It's not because you don't drive me crazy in the most beautiful way
I've just never been taught how to speak this way
My love has never been accepted this way
My kind words, and good intentions have all been thrown away
And I know it's not fair to you because it all happened before you even
walked my way
I'll never forget that day
You have changed my life in the best way
I just wish I could get my mouth to connect to my heart the right way
You deserve to know I rock with you the long way
I see you fading in front of me
I wish I could just say sumn'.

Stars

Let the darkness try me
Cause when the night comes down
it's only stars you see

Spill The Beans

I'm not in the habit of telling anybody
everything
I don't think anyone should have all of the beans
and part of me wonders if it's gotten in between God and me

Point The Finger 1

I don't blame you, today.

The protective parts of me feel shame.

My mind loops versions of a past and hopes of a future that are non-existent.

Maybe it's self-important, but I can't help feeling

I am the one to blame.

We

When people talk about their best friends I miss you
I don't think that will ever change
We spent so much time pouring into each other
Even when miles apart grew we spent time together

We
We gave so much love
We acknowledged our fate
We pledged that we belonged
We'd encourage one another

We

Be Yourself

Today will be what it will be
Be sure to be who you truly are
And if tomorrow comes you can glory
Knowing you never took down

Between Us Two

Then things changed and I don't know if you felt it too
The shift in the atmosphere when the rift grew
Between us two
I can pinpoint the moment you no longer felt like you
I'm stuck longing to hear what's new
I just want one call with the truth

Heartache lingers beneath the surface
I can feel the miles apart in this cavern
Between us two
Our time apart is growing
Our separation is showing
Yet I don't have any answers
Nor fruit to reap from our time sowing

Who Turned Out The Lights?

You walked right up to me and stole my sight
And if I hadn't have spoken up
You'd have tried to make off with everything I have to offer
Ohhh but you weren't quick enough
Even with my sight gone I could feel something wasn't right
I evaded your devious plans before I stayed another night
Your kind thinks it's so clever
You think you have it all figured out
And because I couldn't see, I had to go off what I heard
Those silky words sounded good, but I could feel something wasn't right
you attempted to beguile me with inside jokes and a smooth voice
I laughed so haaaaardddd my sides hurt!
Mouth wide open, head knocked back
I cackled and guffawed as if I'd just discovered what it meant to laugh
It seemed like a good time but I could feel something wasn't right
And right when it seemed you had me in your clutches
I remembered the importance of my intuition
although under these hands you're a work of art
Feelings go beyond tactile in matters of life or death
My survival depends on my ability to listen to that voice inside of me
For all the time you stood tangibly in front of me
you were never truly there
All the moments I spent loaning you parts of me
they were never meant to be yours
Not for a month, or a season, in fact
your subscription has been revoked and I no longer wish to serve you
Your services are no longer needed
allat
So I'll be on my merry way
I'm sure the light will guide me

You may have stole my eyes,
But I'd rather walk by faith

Point The Finger 2

You've made me question everything

You've carved a hole in my heart

You walked towards a new beginning

You cemented our chapter's end with your new start.

(simple as that)

You can never be replaced.

A message from Vania

Thank you for taking the time to read this work. If you enjoyed it, please take the time to leave a review or share your thoughts on any of the poems. Whether it's a little or a lot, I'd love to hear it. Your interpretations, and takeaways could carry someone through a tough moment - or we can celebrate your victories, echoed in these words, together!

Feel free to join in on the excitement:

Instagram: @_allinav
Facebook: Vania Alane Copeland
TikTok: Myfathershairiswoolytoo

You are loved!

-Vania Copeland

Made in the USA
Columbia, SC
14 September 2024

42084310R00043